The Power of Correspondence

Professional Writing Strategies for Public Administrators

Ygnacio "Nash" Flores, EdD
LCDR/MACS USN (Ret)

The Power of Correspondence

Professional Writing Strategies for Public Administrators

Ygnacio "Nash" Flores, EdD
LCDR/MACS USN (Ret)

Contents

Preface

During my forty years of serving in the Navy, working in community-college administration, and teaching in colleges and universities, I have realized the value of effective writing in a professional environment. Writing professionally is a skill developed through patience and practice. To refine your skills and become an accomplished writer, write as much as possible. In this guide I provide examples of correspondence that I have used over the years in the Navy, academia, and my private life.

The examples I provide in this guide are far from being definitive as the only way to write memos or papers. When writing professionally, follow the guidance of the organization's practices in correspondence unless you can convince them otherwise.

Decades ago, when I complained about policy, I received the advice: if you do not like the policy, write the policy the way you envision it. Since then, I have written or amended directives, instructions, police reports, admiralty investigations, administrative investigations, legal briefs, board polices, bargaining agreements, and much more. I give this advice to you too. The power of writing professionally is limitless. Look for opportunities to write as much as possible. Write, write, write!

PART ONE
Basic Writing Tips

Basic Writing Tips

Writing is one of the strongest means of communication, and all kinds of professional depend on it. Everyone has some background in writing academic papers and personal communication, but professional writing differs from these.

As a professional, you will write various memoranda, letters, reports, and presentations. All this professional correspondence requires you to write clearly and concisely with a writing style that does not confuse or lose the attention of the reader. Poor grammar and superfluous information must be avoided.

Guidelines to follow, include:

- Since the goal of a good writer is to effectively deliver the intended message, you must keep in mind many factors about your intended audience, including who they are and what their professional or academic level is. Some general principles of effective writing include: Use an outline to organize your narrative

- Keep your writing focused on your message's objective

- Have a clear structure to your correspondence
    - If required, use mandated templates
    - Use headings to identify important concept and to organize your correspondence
    - Each sentence needs to support the preceding and proceeding sentences in a logical argument
    - Each paragraph needs to support the preceding and proceeding paragraphs in a logical argument
    - Use appendices to add additional information to your narrative without making the body of your correspondence too lengthy
    - Use a recognized method of citing sources you used to support your correspondence

- Use short, simple words and sentences
- Use one thought for each sentence
- Use a clear writing style that is easy to follow and consistent throughout the correspondence
- Use correct grammar
- Use an active voice instead of a passive voice
- Use parallel grammatical structure for similar or related ideas

Avoid the following writing habits:

- Having an unorganized narrative
- Using complex and difficult to understand words. You will not impress your reader if they must frequently look up words to understand their meaning.
- Using unique argot or acronyms. Introduce all acronyms before using them in your narrative.
- Assuming the reader knows as much as you know
- Using text-speak and emojis
- Typing in all capital letters, bolded statements, underlined words, or overuse of italicized words for emphasis
- Using different fonts, font sizes, or font colors to get attention
- Using long, run-on sentences and paragraphs. A typical sentence should be about twenty words. Restructure paragraphs that are longer than ten lines of text. It is better to have shorter sentences with single ideas housed in paragraphs and subparagraphs.

Active Voice Versus Passive Voice

Using active voice in writing reflects professional writing style. Passive voice has less of an impact on the reader and can create ambiguity in the document's message. An active voice identifies who is doing the action and identifies the primary point of the correspondence.

Example—Active voice: The Chief of Police will take administrative action once the investigation is complete.

The Chief of Police does the action.

Avoid passive voice.

Example—Passive voice: Administrative action will be taken by the Chief of Police once the investigation is complete.

Example—Active voice: Deputy Chiefs will implement this policy starting next month.

Deputy Chiefs do the action.

Avoid passive voice.

Example—Passive voice: This policy will be implemented by Deputy Chiefs starting next month.

Passive voice often does not identify who is acting in the narrative and makes the sentence longer and the message less direct. Passive sentences often include a phrase with the word "by." However, there are times when passive voice is preferred. When the focus of the sentence should be on what is done, rather than who does it, passive voice is appropriate.

Parallel Grammatical Structure

Parallel structure means using a similar pattern of words, phrases, clauses or syntax within a sentence, group of sentences, items in a list, set of headings, etc. It's main function is to create consistency that can be relied on so that the reader knows how things relate to one another. For example, when all heading twos are structured alike, the reader knows how important the sections are in relation to heading one and heading three.

Example—Parallel Structure:

Standard Operating Procedures 19-003-b:

   a. Establishes policy and assigns responsibilities for the Body Worn Camera program within the Department

   b. Cancels Standard Operating Procedures 19-003-a

Example—Parallel Structure:

Standard Operating Procedures 19-003-b:

    a. Establishes new policy and assigns responsibilities for the Body Worn Camera program within the Department

    b. Standard Operating Procedures 19-003-a is hereby canceled and superseded

Regulatory Verbs

Punitive ordinances, directives, and instructions require verbs that direct mandatory action. Punitive documents hold employees and citizens responsible for non-compliance. Choose your words carefully to communicate the level of obligation you intend.

Examples—Punitive verbs:

- To denote a mandatory action, use *must*.
- To denote a future required action, use *will*.

Examples—Non-punitive verbs that allow a person discretion about whether to comply:

- To denote an optional action, use *may*.
- To denote an optional action, use *can*.
- To denote an optional action, use *should*.

Tips on Writing Style

This section of the guide uses the writing style prescribed by the American Psychological Association (APA). The Publication Manual of the American Psychological Association (APA Manual) provides the primary guidance on writing in the APA style.

While professional writing does not normally use a specific writing style, the summary below captures some of the everyday rules you will need to know to professionalize your writing style. These guidelines provide you with the necessary direction for your writing assignments.

However, the preferences of your managerial staff or other governing instructions will supersede the specific format and writing requirements in this guide. (The foremost difference between APA and professional styles shows up at the start of a long document. Scientific writing often requires an abstract, but government-related writing requires an executive summary.)

Documents:

- Manuscripts are typed or printed on 8½ by 11" white-bond paper.

- Typeface: The preferred fonts for reports are Times New Roman or Courier. Avoid using flamboyant fonts such as *Brush Script* or **GOUDY STOUT**.

- Font size: Use 12-point type unless directed to use a different size.

- Line spacing: Write text in single-spaced format, including the list of references, unless directed to do otherwise.

- Margins: Margins should be one inch on all sides. If you plan to bind your document, you need to reset the left margin to 1.5 inches.

- Alignment: Left align your text. Do not use full or right justification anywhere in your document, including for block quotations.

- Paragraph indentation: Indent the first line of a paragraph half an inch from the left margin. It is best to use the Tab Key one click. Some documents use block paragraphs with no indentation. Whichever you use, be consistent throughout your document.

- Parts of the document: Normally, your document includes:

  o Title page

  o Executive summary (abstract) if required

  o Body of document

  o References

- Tables of Contents: Use the Table of Contents tool in the References section of Word to create a table of contents. Do not try and type one in freestyle. Freestyle tables of contents rarely align well and look extremely sloppy.

- Acronyms: If you need to use an acronym make sure you introduce it to the reader the first time you use it in your narrative. It is important to note that an acronym can have more than one meaning. See the example below:

  We went to the Center for Interactive Activities (CIA) to look at examples that could improve our own processes. The CIA stressed individuality as part of the process.

- Abbreviations: It is best to avoid colloquial abbreviations in your document. Not every reader will understand what your abbreviations stand for. See the example below:

  Offs. Jones and Hernandez responded to the call before returning to HQ.

- Contractions: It is best not to use any contractions in your writing. While the use of contractions has gained in acceptance, it is best to write out each word you use. Misused contractions can confuse your reader. See the examples below:

  o You're car was left abandoned in the park. This should be written: Your car was left abandoned in the park.

  o The suspect carried it's illegal gains in his pocket. This should be written: The suspect carried its illegal gains in his pocket.

o They're, their, and there often get misused. Which sentence below is correct?

- Their all criminals.

- They're all criminals.

- There all criminals

The middle sentence is correct.

Titles and Headings

Do not bold titles unless directed to do so. Follow the same guidance for underlining and using italics. Titles and headings designate major themes of your document, which provide the reader with a means of quick reference. They also frame how individuals read and understand your document.

Use no more than five levels of headings, though it is doubtful you will need all five in any document you write. Normally, the introduction to a document does not require a heading to identify the section.

Proofreading

Proofreading is the final step before presenting your document for a review or submitting it for distribution and/or publication. Pay attention to correcting grammatical errors and spelling mistakes not caught by the word-processing-review functions. Errors and minor mechanical problems can distract or lose the reader.

Tips for proofreading:

- Read a printed copy of your document, rather than reading from the screen.

- Read your document aloud or have a friend read it to you.

- Read your document line by line and move a ruler under each line.

- Read versions of your document side-by-side, and compare them.

- Read your document backward.
- Have a trusted colleague review and/or edit your document.

Pagination: All pages, including the title page, should have Arabic numerals in the header section. The running head of the document and page number should be consistent throughout the document.

Spacing after Punctuation: Type one space after periods, question marks, commas, colons, and semicolons.

Italics: Use italics to identify the titles of all books, magazines, journals, and other creative works.

Citing Sources

Writers are often confused about whether to give credit in their writing for outside inspiration or influence. Although some gray areas certainly exist, many guidelines are available to provide writers with an adequate understanding of proper documentation. Failing to cite a source could result in a claim of plagiarism against you.

As a rule, a writer cites anything or anyone that provided inspiration or knowledge during the process of researching for and/or writing a document. Unfortunately, it is sometimes difficult to determine what is a truly unique idea or generated from one's own thoughts and what has been borrowed from another source. If a student has any doubt about the originality of an idea, the safest choice always is to acknowledge the appropriate source. Do not cite common knowledge—such as, the sun rises in the east. Likewise, a mere reference to a publication by name, with no information quoted, paraphrased, or summarized, does not require citation.

Citation in an academic paper takes place in two different areas in APA style. The first is the "References" section at the end of your paper. The second is citing references within your narrative.

For professional writing, footnotes provide a reference for the reader without making your document look like an academic paper. Check with your organization to see if they require citations via footnote or if they want sources cited within the narrative of your text.

Examples of quotes:

> The photographic industry has made great strides over the last few decades; however, "the iPhone has had the largest impact in making available to the novice photographer tools of a professional quality (Mason, 2015, p. 23)".

Or

> Mason (2015) has stated "the photographic industry has made great strides over the last few decades; however, "the iPhone has had the largest impact in making available to the novice photographer tools of a professional quality (p. 23)".

Use of quotes should be no more than one or two sentences. Direct quotes larger than this have the following format:

- The change in the photographic professions is dynamic as posited by Mason (2015) who stated:

> "The photographic industry has made great strides over the last few decades; however, the iPhone has had the largest impact in making available to the novice photographer tools of a professional quality. The many photographic awards given to the everyday photographer using his or her iPhone or Android to capture stunning pictures of a level not possible 10 or 20 years ago illustrate this capability. The challenge for professional photographers is in differentiation through the skills that an iPhone cannot deliver, such as capturing the subject at perfect angles, timing and photographic manipulation (p. 23)".

Take care not to let block quotes dominate most of the document's narrative. Writers must use their own words in their documents.

Examples of paraphrasing:

> The photographic industry has made great strides over

the last few decades; however, the iPhone has had a significant effect in photography by providing the novice photographer with a camera capable of taking professional quality images (Mason, 2015). [Note: no page number required]

See how I paraphrased the idea I quoted above into 'my' words? This is the preferred method of writing. The rule here is: If you get an idea from someone, give him or her credit.

The best advice for any writer is: "When in doubt, cite!"

Use an Authoritative Voice

Use an authoritative voice in your correspondence that is based on facts and logic. Avoid using your documents to rant or complain as if you were standing on a soapbox or talking to a friend. Avoid biased or partial writing. Ranting in a memo will lose your reader very quickly, and it will detract from your professionalism. I call these voices: standing on a soapbox and standing at a lectern.

Example—Standing on a Soapbox:

> The team leader made poor decisions, which we all knew were wrong, and we had no choice but to follow him into failure or to get placed on report.

Example—Unbiased Statement; Standing at a Lectern:

> The team leader, a Baby Boomer, made decisions in a strict chain of command that reinforced the inflexibility of generational leadership discussed by Dimock (2019). This form of decision making, reinforced by Taylor's (2019) perspectives on the conflict of subordinate team leaders who were Millennials. The law enforcement team, like a military unit, mirrored the aspects of duty discussed in the Marine Corps Values (2008). This resulted in the injury of two law enforcement officers.

Notes

PART TWO
How to Write an Effective Memo

How to Write an Effective Memo

Memoranda—or memo—form an important part of daily professional communication. Memos relay information between two or more parties, to create a record, and to provide direction. I will briefly cover five types of memos commonly used by public safety professionals. They are:

- The Memorandum For
- The Memorandum for the Record
- The Informal Memo
- The Briefing Memo
- Memorandum of Understanding/Memorandum of Agreement

Each type of memo has a unique type of information to communicate between two or more people. Normally memos provide a means to communicate between parts of an organization. They also facilitate communication between organizations, such as one police department to another police department, or between a police chief and another department head in the city. All memos are records of administrative actions. One caution for a leader to exercise is that a leader needs to avoid *leading by memo*. When a memo is not appropriate, public safety professionals use other forms of writing. Part 3 of this guide discusses these papers and reports.

I wrote this section from the perspective that you are a leader in a public-safety organization. Research and drafting memos with your thoughts, ideas, and opinions is part of your job as a leader. Memos allow you to communicate a variety of ideas in a concise and professional manner. Because memos request or share important information, exercise care to ensure your message is clear and accurate. A poorly written memo can confuse readers, offend employees, and cost time.

Even with the popularity of email and teleconferencing, effective memo-writing remains an essential skill for public-safety leaders involved with interoffice communications. Typically, memos are short and communicate a single subject. Frequently, they are delivered by email, but they must follow the same professional and formatting standards as memos printed on paper.

Writing a memo is not difficult and does not require much time, though it must be concise and to the point, just the facts. Remember—even though it is often conveyed electronically—a memo is a written document, which makes it an official record.

Your memo represents you and your agency. Any glaring errors may cast you in a negative light among your peers and subordinates. You never know who may read your memo. Once distributed, it's nearly impossible to recall a memo. Writing with the mindset that the Supreme Court of the United States will review your memo is a good way to discipline your writing.

Key Points in Memo Writing

- *Pre-planning.* Make a list of your key points. Write a draft before you complete your final memo.

- *Identify Your Purpose Quickly.* Discuss the main point of the memo in the first paragraph.

- *Know your Audience.* Use respectful and proper tone in your narrative. Use caution so that memos, such as the Informal Memo, do not use inappropriate language.

- *Formatting is Important.* Use a standard format throughout your memo. Formatting may include headings, bullets, and use of font.

- Limiting each paragraph to one idea. If a one-paragraph idea seems too long, see if you can make your point more precise or try to create two paragraphs, with each paragraph communicating a unique point.

- *Signature Line.* Depending on the memo developed, you may sign it with a full signature or initial your name in the *From* line in the memo. Formal memos should conclude with a signature. Make sure to date all memos.

- *Copy To.* When required, route a copy to the appropriate office or officer. List the Copy To addressees at the end of the memo so that the recipient is aware of who else has received or is going to receive the memo.

- *Clear, Concise, and Accurate.* Memos should usually be no more than one page in length. In certain circumstances, appendices, tabs, or other supporting material may accompany the memo. Make sure you identify attachments in the memo's narrative.

Notes

Basic Format for a Memorandum

Most of the memos you write will follow the basic format of presenting your point clearly and concisely. Correspondence requiring more than one page is best written in reports and papers as explained in Part 3 of this guide.

MEMORANDUM

Date

To: Recipient's name, title
From: Author's name, title

Subj: PRIMARY TOPIC OF MEMO

1. State the purpose of your memo clearly in the first paragraph.

2. Support your argument.

3. Conclude your memo with a closing statement or recommendations.

Sincerely,

Y. Flores

Example of a Basic Memo Format

The Memorandum For

The Memorandum For is the most formal memo. Use this type when communicating with the senior-most officials in an organization. An example is a Chief responding to a query by the Mayor or City Manager.

Expect a Memorandum For to receive high visibility, since more than the recipient will read it. If routing this memo through a chain of command, ensure you address all officials in the proper order of precedence. A good way to lose support is to be discourteous to an administrator in your chain of command.

For maximum effect, the memorandum for is written on formal letterhead stationery. End your memo with a formal identification section that includes your typed name, title, and signature.

MEMORANDUM FOR DEPUTY AND DIVISION CHIEFS

October 21, 2016

Subj: SERGEANT TEST 2016

Ref: (a) Department Operations Manual
        (b) Officer's Union 343, Collective Bargaining Unit Agreement 2015-2017

1. The 2016 Sergeant Test will take place on November 16, 2016 at the Regional Training Center at 0800 hours.

2. Ensure all qualified patrol officers complete a candidate application for the Sergeant Test per references (a) and (b) and submit them to Lieutenant Garcia in the administrative office by 1600 hours on November 4, 2016.

3. Deputy and Division Chiefs will meet on November 21, 2016 in my conference room to rank the candidate patrol officers for future interviews scheduled on January 18 and 19, 2017.

4. Deputy and Division Chiefs will brief on the performance and administrative records for patrol officers in their areas during the ranking of candidate officers.

5. Refer any administrative questions to Lieutenant Garcia.

6. I look forward to a very competitive process this year as we have fewer open sergeant positions than we have qualified officers.

Sincerely,

T.Q. Alvarez
Chief of Police

Example of a Memorandum For

The Memorandum for the Record

The Memorandum for the Record memorializes a significant event as an official record. For example, this kind of memo is used when capturing key decisions made in a meeting. Memoranda for the Record are official sources of information for future reference.

Another example use is capturing an event that does not require a police report but warrants an official record. Using the Memorandum for the Record is also a good way to record what took place in meetings with those outside of your organization. I refer to these memos as a CYA (cover your ass) memos.

While the purpose of this memo serves as a record of an event, routing a copy of the memo to a superior for notification purposes is acceptable. The Memorandum for the Record is a valuable form of in-house correspondence.

MEMORANDUM FOR THE RECORD

May 17, 2010

From: Sergeant Miller, Southwest Division

Subj: PERFORMANCE IMPROVEMENT PLAN FOR OFFICER NEIL

Encl: (a) Performance Improvement Plan ICO Officer Sandy Neil

1. On May 17, 2010, I met with Officer Neil concerning her performance and the Performance Improvement Plan (PIP) submitted by Neil's RTO, Corporal Aziz. Officer Neil is aware of her shortcomings in being assertive while on patrol and has a genuine desire to become a police officer.

2. I approved the PIP submitted by Corporal Aziz and scheduled for Officer Neil to attend Scenario Training in June 2010.

3. I made it clear to Officer Neil that this was her last opportunity to complete the RTO training and that further substandard performance would result in her dismissal from the department.

R. K. Miller

CC: Captain Sissoko

Example of a Memorandum For the Record

The Informal Memo

The informal memo is the most commonly used memo within an organization. This memo facilitates routine communication among most members in an organization. Before email, informal memos used preprinted memo sheets and facilitated the writing of short handwritten messages. Preprinted memos saved on paper with their smaller-than-standard-sized letter forms.

MEMORANDUM

February 5, 2009

To: Sergeant Smith
From: Sergeant Hatamy

Subj: COUNTY FAIR

1. I will be assigning three officers to work the morning shift and one to work on evening shift on opening day. I am aware you will have two officers on morning shift and two officers on evening shift for opening day. Which shift do you want to take? Morning or evening? Check the shift you want and I will submit the schedule to the LT.

Respectfully,

T. Hatamy

_____ Morning Shift

_____ Evening Shift

Example of an Informal Memo

The Briefing Memo

The briefing Memo informs a wider audience within an organization. Some organizations refer to this memo as an executive memo, decision paper, or summary/fact sheet. The Briefing Memo establishes important operational and administrative actions.

MEMORANDUM FOR Mayor Knoll

June 9, 1999

From: Big Jefe, Chief of Police
       Pasha Bei, Fire Chief

Subject: IMPLEMENTATION OF A WELLNESS PROGRAM

Purpose: To obtain funding to implement a Wellness Program for all personnel in the City's Police and Fire Departments.

Discussion: Over the last three years the city has experienced an active shooter at the local mall that killed two people and wounded sixteen others along with two wildfires that killed one person and caused the destruction of personal property over twenty million dollars. While our First Responders performed admirably in these and other calls for services, we have noted the following effects on our personnel:

1. Three police officers have suffered from PTSD with one committing suicide.
2. Four firefighters have suffered from PTSD.
3. 456 hours of sick time were stress related.
4. Five personnel divorced.
5. The rate of personnel grievances went up 12% and disciplinary action increased 27%.

A movement in public safety agencies is addressing similar issues by taking care of the health of the body and mind through Wellness Programs that reduce stress and increase understanding of the challenges our officers and staff face in the line of duty (Appendix A).

The investment in a Wellness Program can save the lives of our personnel as well as reduce the costs of experiencing negative side effects of the trauma experienced by our officers and staff.

Recommendation: Authorize the implement a Wellness Program based on the mindfulness techniques described by the National Training Forum (Appendix B). The first year of the program will cost $50,000 that will need to come from the general budget. We will program future expenses as standalone line items in our budgets.

Big Jefe   Pasha Bei

Example of a Briefing Memo

Memorandum of Understanding/ Memorandum of Agreement

Many organizations enter into agreements and partnerships that require a means of identifying specific services and activities between the cooperative parties. Two of the most common forms of these agreements are Memorandum of Understanding [MOU] and Memorandum of Agreement [MOA]. However, many professionals frequently misuse these memoranda, so it's important to be clear which form the circumstances require.

An MOU is an agreement based on a common purpose. It is not a legally binding document. The MOU details common services and activities between the parties involved *without* the parties entering into the binding power of a contract. The MOU details mutual expectations between the parties. A successfully implemented MOU may serve as the framework for an MOA.

Conversely, an MOA is more formal than the MOU. The MOA can serve as a legally binding document between the parties involved. The MOA is a limited and conditional commitment and agreement to cooperate. The MOA usually contains detail that links services to funding sources.

As with most memos, there is no one overarching format. The example below uses articles to organize the understandings of the MOU.

MEMORANDUM OF UNDERSTANDING
BETWEEN
RIVER CITY SCHOOL DISTRICT AND FOOTHILL SHERIFF DEPARTMENT
FOR YEARS
2010-2012

Article I: **Purpose.**
River City School District (RCSD) has been negatively impacted by the rise in crime experienced throughout the county for the last eighteen months. The rise in crime has been centered around school venues. The Foothill Sheriff Department (FSD) ...
are co...
the la...

State law XXX, details procedures on the exchange of information between school administrators and law enforcement officials relating to criminal acts occurring in a school zone. State law YYYY, further delineates the relationship between school administrators and law enforcement officials in a designated Safe School Zone. These laws provide procedures for information sharing concerning any juvenile, police records relating to juveniles, or other relevant information when such information relates to criminal conduct and delinquency or suspected criminal activity and suspected delinquency, or conduct covered by state laws XXX and YYYY which would classify a student as a child in need of protection or other social and health services.

Article II: **Effec...**
This N...
agreem...
this M...
This N...

Article VII: **Reporting Procedures.**
To the extent possible, oral and written reports required by this MOU shall include:

    (a) Identification of the criminal act or suspected criminal act;
    (b) The name and address, if known, of any person(s) suspected of committing a criminal act. If the ...
    the re...
    (c) The n...
    act. I...
    or gu...

    (c) *School Employee.* Any district administrator, teacher, or other employee to include part-time, contract services, and volunteers acting on behalf of the district.
    (d) *School Purposes.* Classroom instruction, school-sponsored programs, and any educational or extracurricular activities performed under the umbrella of the RCSD.

Article III: **Invol...**
This a...
and th...
provid...
staff, ...
(MOU...
Initiat...

Article IV: **Requi...**
In acc...
who h...
safe sc...
distric...
such r...
an aut...

The written r...
officials if th...
results in a w...

Nothing in this MOU shall limit events that may be reported to law enforcement officials or to limit RCSD employees from requesting law enforcement assistance on matters not discussed in this MOU.

Article V: **Admi...**
The R...
for em...
or an ...
princi...
Admi...

Article VIII: **Reportable...**
Pursuant to s...
regardless of...
    (a) Unifo...
    (b) Natio...
    (c) Addit...
    added...
    the FS...
    refere...

Article X: **Investigations.**
Law enforcement officials will conduct investigations on RCSD property per state law. Collection of evidence and interviews will be done in accordance with applicable state law governing law enforcement activities and the State Education Code governing law enforcement activities on school property.

Article XI: **Training.**
The RCSD and FSD will form a joint training cadre to provide employees with initial and ongoing training relative to this MOU and its purpose.

Article VI: **Confi...**

Article IX: **Definitions.**
Per applicabl...
MOU:
    (a) *Safe ...*
    buses...
    (b) *Schoo...*
    RCSD...
    buses...

Article XII. **Communication.**
The RCSD and FSD agree to maintain regular, open, and effective communication to measure the effect of this MOU. Upon mutual written agreement, parties may recommend improvements to this MOU and make modifications to these Articles as necessary to meet the intent of this agreement.

Signed: _____   Signed: _____
Knowzit Tal, PhD   Nixel J. Powers
Superintendent, River City School District   Foothill Sheriff

Example of an MOU

PART THREE
Reports and Papers

Reports and Papers

Correspondence used in a professional setting requires more than writing a good memo. Professional papers, official reports, and administrative investigations are types of correspondence, which are written in more detail than a memo provides. This section of the guide provides guidance on developing the following:

- Bottom Line Up Front [BLUF]
- Point Paper
- Talking Paper
- White Paper
- Trip Report
- After-Action/Lessons Learned Report (AAR)

BLUF

There are many times when a memo or a formal paper or report is too much information for a person to read. In these situations, providing a paragraph that surmises the entirety of a report or issue is best for the writer and audience. This truncated form of writing is known as a BLUF, which stands for *bottom line up front*, or the practice of placing the conclusions and recommendations at the front of a report or paper. A BLUF differs from an abstract, summary, or an executive summary in that it is more concise and portrays the document's objective and does not discuss the arguments of the topic. A BLUF is usually no more than one paragraph long.

The County Sheriff's Department is part of the solution to deal with homelessness in the region. The idea of arresting our way out of the homeless problem is a mindset from the previous century. The County Sheriff's Department, along with other law enforcement and public safety agency partners must work proactively and collaboratively with the Health and Human Services Department, educational districts, housing authorities, and public-private partnerships to develop a safe community that addresses homelessness in an ethical, human, and professional manner. The solution to homelessness is a whole of community approach that ensures residents are provided with the opportunity for health services, a safe environment, and personal security.

Example of a BLUF

Point Paper

Point papers are more direct than a standard letter and provide more information than a memo. Point papers focus on *one topic* and provide a list of significant facts and ideas regarding the subject. Point papers provide a means of speaking to an audience with clear, accurate, and consistent information. Point papers also provide a forum to respond to inquiries and requests for information.

Point papers are effective correspondence to submit a recommendation to your superiors. The objective of a point paper is to convince the paper's audience to act by providing the main points with clear recommendations at the end of the paper.

Point Paper for City Council of Big City

Chief Rickman
Chief Big City Fire Department
November 19, 2010

THE GROWTH OF BIG CITY AND PLANNED CONSTRUCTION REQUIRES A NEW
FIRE STATION

Background. Big City has grown in the last ten years adding 15,000 new residents with current
and planned construction of one thousand new residents. Most of the city's expansion is in the
newly incorporated section of northeast Big City. Last year's Backroad Wildfire caused damage
to the northeast section of Big City that cost over $23 million and the death of three people. Not
having a fire station in the northeast of the city prevented a means of quickly responding to the
fire.

Discussion. Constructing and funding a new one-story fire station is within the means of the
City's current budget, though it would be prudent to pursue a bond measure for funding some or
all the costs of purchasing the fire vehicles and equipment above that covered by the Mello-Roos
funding. Cost estimates for what would be Fire Station No.3 are:

- Construction. One story, 14' high, 6,000 square feet, decorative concrete block and
  bearing walls.
- Union labor, contractor fees, architectural fees is $110,000,000.
- Fire engine and equipment: $1,300,000.
- Fire truck with ladder: $800.000.
- Water tanker: $500,000.
- Total estimated cost for Fire Station and vehicles: $112.6 million.
- Staffing of Fire Station No.3 is already programed into the City's five-year plan.

Recommendations. The following actions will provide all communities in Big City with the
means to respond to emergencies and disasters within minutes of a call:

1. Approve the construction of Fire Station No.3 with current funding reserves held by the city.
2. Began the process to have an initiative added to the next election cycle authorizing a bond
   measure to assess homeowners and new construction to support funding the additional costs
   of equipping and maintaining Fire Station No.3.

Example of a Point Paper

Talking Paper

The talking paper provides the audience key points to use when talking in an official capacity. Often you will prepare a talking paper for a superior that will use it to discuss a matter with city or elected officials, community groups, and other organizations. The speaker does not usually have the time to read a detailed report—that is the job of their staff. A talking paper is a good way to provide the speaker with enough of the facts to speak with knowledge and authority.

Talking Paper for Mayor Biggens

July 4, 2001

Subj: OFFICER INVOLVED SHOOTING AT CYCLE PARK

Background:

- Three officers and one deputy responded to a domestic violence incident at Cycle Park at 9:15 pm on July 4, 2001.
- A male individual—the suspect—was holding a gun to the head of his spouse.
- Officers talked the suspect into dropping his gun.
- The suspect then pulled a knife from his back pocket and started to raise it when an officer shot the suspect hitting him in the upper torso.
- Officers arrested suspect and transported him to County Medical Center for treatment.
- Suspect is under police control.
- The spouse is at County Medical Center for observation.

Talking Points:

- There was an officer involved shooting (OIS) earlier in the evening at Cycle Park.
- The suspect had threated another person with a weapon.
- The names of the suspect, victim, and officers are currently confidential.
- The suspect is under arrest receiving medical attention.
- The victim is receiving medical attention.
- No other injuries are known at this time.
- City Police Department is conducting an ongoing investigation.

Summary:

- City police department is conducting ongoing investigation.
- Direct inquires to city Public Affairs Office.

Example of a Talking Paper

White Paper

A white paper is an authoritative document, which informs the reader of a specific topic. For a white paper to be effective, the writer must conduct research into the issue. A white paper provides an expert perspective to the issue. The primary purpose of the white paper is *to inform the reader of an issue* based on your arguments and recommendations.

White papers aid the reader in understanding an issue, solving a problem, or making a decision. Write white papers in a formal tone. White papers contain factual data, detailed narratives, and logical findings and recommendations.

The main audiences you will address in a white paper are one or more of the following stakeholders:

- Strategic
- Technical
- User

The organization of a white paper is important. Start by describing the big picture, and end with your recommendations or solutions. Using headings enables the reader to effectively scan your document. Many white papers are written in block paragraphs.

In the example provided for this correspondence, note the following headings that organize the report:

- Cover Page
- Table of Contents
- Executive Summary—this is like an abstract for a college paper
- Previous Technology in Law Enforcement—this section is the background of the issue being investigated—the problem space—up to the point of the study
  - o **New and Emerging Technologies**—this section shows what your study found that will affect the future of the problem space

o **Conclusions**—a summary of your white paper and the significant findings you identified

o **Recommendations**—what you think needs to happen to make the issues better

o **References**—can also be a Works Cited or Bibliography. It is best to use copyright footnotes in the body of the text and a full citation in the references section.

o **Appendices**—can provide a means of adding important information if the reader requires additional detail on topics presented in the report

Technology in Law Enforcement

Chief Samuel Lightfoot
Community Police Chief

11111 Main Street
Small City, CA.

Executive Summary

Technology is changing the way we live our lives. Enforcing the law has experienced many changes due to technological advances. Technology does not provide law enforcement with cart blanche auth... Amendments... *attention of r...*

Introduction

The US Supreme Court of the United States (SCOTUS) has recognized that technology has outpaced many concepts of privacy in their ruling in *Carpenter v. U.S.* (Appendix A). Keeping our policies aligned with Constitutional rights has been a challenge in the past three years.

Technology is not as bound to the Constitution as is our police department. The .... [*Illustrate the issue so that the reader can make an informed decision based on facts.*]

[*The length of your white paper depends on the complexity of the issue explored. The narrative of the paper focuses on key points of information. Use appendices to provide in-depth reading of issues you introduce in the paper.*]

Previous Technology in Law Enforcement

The use of te
police in Bri
exploring.]

New and E

The fourth i
society. Con
you are expl...

Small City P
adhering to t
public. Smal

Conclusion

Technology
white paper
_____
[2] Doe, J (1999|

Recommendations

Implementing these measures requires the entire city to collaborate .... [*Describe how the solution and recommendations will come to life.*]

References

List the sources you used to develop your white paper. Follow a standardized format for citing sources.

Appendices

List all appendices referred to in the body of the white paper.

Example of a White Paper

Trip Report

A Trip Reports is a necessary tool for recording the use of travel funds. Over the years, Trip Reports have gained the reputation of a task most travelers wish to avoid. Submit them in memo format. The audience of a Trip Report can vary but usually includes operational, training, and fiscal managers. A Trip Report conveys the reason for the trip, primary take-away, and the value of the travel to the organization.

Trip Report

August 11, 1007

To: Chief of Police
From: LT J. Antar, Northeast Division
Via: Chief Fentel, Northeast Division

Subj: TRIP REPORT: INTERNATIONAL ASSOCIATION OF CHIEFS OF POLICE (IACP) CONFERENCE, SAN DIEGO, CA

Attachments: (a) IACP Agenda
              (b) Presentation on Gang Suppression Efforts by LT Antar

Purpose.   Make presentation to general assembly on Gang Suppression Efforts by City of Pear.

Highlights.

- Presentation attended by over 250 IACP participants.
- Panel member on Gang Suppression breakout session.
- Attended workshops on Body Worn Cameras, Technology and the 4th Amendment, and Recruiting the Next Generation Officer.

Unresolved
Issues: IACP representatives requested a follow-up presentation at next year's IACP conference. I was unable to commit to the request.

Action Items. Chief Smalls of Big City Police Department wants to send a team to observe our gang suppression efforts. Chief Smalls requested we send an officer to Big City for one month to train their gang suppression task force.

Value to
Department: Presentation and sitting as an expert on the panel for gang suppression emphasized the vision and efforts of City of Pear. The IACP conference facilitated networking with colleagues from law enforcement agencies from North America, Europe, and Oceania.

Opinions: City of Pear needs to send annual representatives to the IACP Conference.

Very Respectfully

LT. J. Antar

Example of a Trip Report

After Action Report [AAR] and Lessons Learned Report [LLR]

An AAR contains an LLR. Both reports provide post-event analysis of actions taken during the event. An AAR uses existing plans, operating procedures, orders, and objectives issued to an organization against the actions taken in the event.

The intent of an AAR/LLR is not to place blame on an individual. Rather it looks for ways to improve processes, tactics, and procedures.

This guide will use a modified format recommend by the Federal Emergency Management Agency (FEMA) for AARs assessing exercises [www.fema.gov].

The LLR contains the following information:

- Acknowledges expected goals and objectives of the event/program
- Analyzes organizational roles
- Acknowledges effective actions, practices, and strategies in the event/program
- Assesses real and intangible costs of the event/program
- Compares different courses of action (COA) and the impact of social, political, economic, and cultural factors on the COAs
- Provides actions, practices, and strategies to remedy areas needing improvement

Modified FEMA format for an AAR:

Background of event:

- Event name
- Scope of event
- Date and location of event
- Participating organizations/agencies/organizations
- Mission area(s) and Core Capabilities
- Specific objective of event
- Challenges encountered
- Brief scenario of event
- Principal actors and point of contact (POC)

Executive summary

Event goals and objectives

Analysis of capabilities demonstrated

Findings of actions taken

Recommendations

Conclusions

Improvement Plan (IP) matrix

Additional appendices may include:

- Lessons learned
- A participant feedback summary
- Timeline of event
- List of acronyms
- List of agencies

Example of an AAR Format

Summary

This guide provides a simple approach to develop writing strategies to meet the writing requirements in the professional work environment. The importance of communicating in a professional setting cannot be overstated. A well-written memo, report, or other correspondence can affect an organization's strategy and operations. Strong writing skills will set you apart from others in your organization. I use over 40 years of experience serving in various governmental and public administrative roles to develop the content of this guide. Though the emphasis is on public administration, this guide is helpful to college and university students and business professionals.

About the Author

Dr. Flores is currently on the faculty at Rio Hondo College, serving as the Homeland Security Program Coordinator. He was formerly the Dean of Public Safety and Interim Dean of Business at Rio Hondo College. Dr. Flores is a retired Lieutenant Commander who honorably retired after 27 years of service in the US Navy. Before being commissioned as a naval officer, he served in the Navy as a Senior.

Dr. Flores holds a Doctor of Education (EdD) from the University of Southern California, an MBA from Pepperdine University (Presidents & Key Executives program), an MPS-HS from Pennsylvania State University, a MAIR from the University of San Diego, a Diploma from the Navy War College (Command and Staff program), and a BSCJ National University. Dr. Flores also has an Executive Certificate in Public Policy from Harvard's Kennedy School of Government and a Professional Certificate from the University of Maryland, University College in Drones and Autonomous Systems.

Dr. Flores has decades of teaching in professional and academic programs. He has taught courses in criminal justice, criminology, homeland security, public policy, and business at several colleges and universities throughout the United States.

Notes

Notes